Summer Blast

Getting Ready for First Grade

Reading

Math

Writing

Art

Puzzles

and more!

Author
Jodene Smith, M.A.

SHELL EDUCATION

Standards

To learn important shifts in today's standards, see the Parent Handbook on pages 123–128. For information on how this resource meets national and other state standards, scan the QR code or visit our website at http://www.shelleducation.com and following the on-screen directions.

Publishing Credits

Corinne Burton, M.A.Ed., *President*; Emily R. Smith, M.A.Ed., *Content Director*; Jennifer Wilson, *Senior Editor*; Robin Erickson, *Multimedia Designer*; Valerie Morales, *Assistant Editor*; Stephanie Bernard, *Assistant Editor*; Amber Goff, *Editorial Assistant*; Mindy Duits, *Cover Concept*

Image Credits

pp. 5–6, p. 12, p. 15, p. 22: iStock; All other images Shutterstock

Standards

Shell Education

5301 Oceanus Drive
Huntington Beach, CA 92649-1030
http://www.shelleducation.com

ISBN 978-1-4258-1551-6

© 2016 Shell Educational Publishing, Inc.

Table of Contents

Introduction

Welcome Letter 4

Helpful Family Resources 5

Weekly Activities

Week 1 Activities 13

Week 2 Activities 23

Week 3 Activities 33

Week 4 Activities 43

Week 5 Activities 53

Week 6 Activities 63

Week 7 Activities 73

Week 8 Activities 83

Week 9 Activities 93

Appendices

Appendix A: Activity Cards 103

Appendix B: Answer Key 119

Appendix C: Parent Handbook 123

Welcome to Summer Blast!

Dear Family,

Welcome to *Summer Blast: Getting Ready for First Grade*. First grade will be an exciting and challenging year for your child. There will be plenty of new learning opportunities, including writing complete sentences and more work with addition and subtraction! Interesting new topics in science and social studies will help keep your child engaged in the lessons at school.

Summer Blast was designed to help solidify the concepts your child learned in kindergarten and to help your child prepare for the year ahead. The activities are based on today's standards and provide practice with essential skills for the upcoming grade level. Keeping reading, writing, and mathematics skills sharp while your child is on break from school will help his or her first-grade year get off to a great start. This book will help you BLAST through summer learning loss!

Keep these tips in mind as you work with your child this summer:

◆ Set aside a specific time each day to work on the activities.

◆ Have your child complete one or two pages each time he or she works, rather than an entire week's worth of activity pages at one time.

◆ Keep all practice sessions with your child positive and constructive. If the mood becomes tense or you and your child get frustrated, set the book aside and find another time to practice.

◆ Since your child is still an emerging reader, be sure to read the direction for him or her. If your child is having difficulty understanding what to do, work through some of the problems together.

◆ Encourage your child to do his or her best work, and compliment the effort that goes into learning.

Enjoy spending time with your child during his or her vacation from school, and be sure to help him or her prepare for for the next school year. First grade will be here before you know it!

#51551—Summer Blast

What Does Your Rising First Grader Need to Know?

1. Read grade-level books more fluently.

2. Know how to read and spell sight words.

3. Write complete sentences while focusing on capitalization and punctuation.

4. Know how to count up to 100 and be able to read and write the numbers.

5. Add and subtract numbers up to 20.

6. Add and subtract larger numbers without regrouping.

7. Observe and describe things using sight, taste, touch, sound, and smell.

8. Understand habitats for different living things.

9. Understand the responsibilities of being a good citizen.

10. Know the holidays in the United States and the symbols that represent the holidays.

Things to Do as a Family

General Skills

◆ Make sure your child gets plenty of exercise. Children need about 60 minutes of physical activity each day. The summer months are the perfect time to go swimming, ride bicycles, or play outdoor team sports.

◆ It's also important for children this age to get plenty of sleep. Children this age need between 9 and 11 hours of sleep each night. Even in the summer, establish a nightly bedtime routine that involves relaxing activities such as a warm bath or shower or reading a story.

Reading Skills

◆ Help build your child's comprehension skills by asking questions about what they've read. For example, you could ask why he or she thinks a character has done something, or you could ask what he or she thinks will happen next.

◆ Encourage your child to reread his or her favorite books, stories, or poems. Rereading will help your child read more quickly and accurately.

Writing Skills

◆ Have your child keep a daily diary/journal about activities he or she is doing during time off from school. He or she can draw pictures or write words or sentences.

◆ Ask your child to help you write in everyday situations. You can have him or her help you write a grocery list or write a thank-you note.

Mathematics Skills

◆ Ask your child to compare different objects' sizes. For example, have your child put his or her toys in order from biggest to smallest or ask him or her which of two objects is smaller or bigger, etc.

◆ Encourage your child to practice telling time. If you are going to a movie, a special event, or even an appointment, ask your child to help you figure out what time you should leave. For example: If the movie begins at 3:30 P.M. and it takes 15 minutes to get there, what time should we leave? Be sure to point to the clock hands to support your child.

Summer Reading Log

Directions: Keep track of the books you read with your child here!

Date	Title	Number of Pages

Top 5 Family Field Trips

A Trip to a Museum

Your first stop should be the gift shop. Have your child pick out five postcards of artifacts or paintings in the museum. Then, as you visit the museum, your child should be on the lookout for the five items he or she chose. It's an individual scavenger hunt! (Postcards usually have a bit of information about the pictured item to help you find it.) If he or she finds all five, you can celebrate the great accomplishment! Plus, your child gets to keep the postcards as memories of the day.

A Trip to a National Park

The National Park Service has a great program called Junior Rangers. Be sure you check in with the rangers at the visitors' center to see what tasks your child can complete to earn a Junior Ranger patch and/or certificate. Before you travel to the park, your child can also go to the WebRangers site (http://www.nps.gov/webrangers/) and check out your vacation spot, play games, and earn virtual rewards!

A Trip to a Zoo

Before your trip, create a Zoo Bingo card. Include various characteristics that your child should look for (for example, a warm-blooded animal, an animal with feathers, an animal from Africa, etc.). Bring the Zoo Bingo card and a small clipboard with you. As you spend the day exploring, have your child write or draw the name of one animal that fits each category you come across. An animal should only be used for one category/box (for example, a lion cannot be used for both a warm-blooded animal and an animal from Africa). When he or she gets bingo, celebrate the great accomplishment!

A Trip to a Library

Help your child discover new books. First, ask your child what his or her favorite type of story is. For example, "Do you like funny stories or adventure stories better?" Then, choose at least three books that fit that topic or interest. Read the story aloud with your child. As you read, ask your child to explain how the pictures match the text.

A Trip to a Farmers Market

Farmers markets are great places to learn about different fruits and vegetables. Ask your child to help you find the colors of the rainbow. At each fruit or vegetable stand, ask your child to locate one color from the rainbow. Then, explain what the fruit or vegetable is and the different types of recipes it can be used in. For example, a red tomato can be used for ketchup, pizza, pasta sauce, etc.

Top 5 Family Science Labs

Science Fun for Everyone!—Floating Egg

http://www.sciencefun.org/kidszone/experiments/floating-egg/

Learn about density by making an egg float in water.

Science Fun for Everyone!—Polishing Pennies

http://www.sciencefun.org/kidszone/experiments/polishing-pennies/

Learn about oxidation and acid in this clever and easy experiment.

Science Fun—Needle through a Balloon

http://scifun.chem.wisc.edu/homeexpts/needle.htm

Learn how long molecules help keep a balloon from popping.

Science Bob—Add Color to Flowers Using Science

https://sciencebob.com/color-flowers-using-science/

Learn how flowers use water as you change the petal colors.

Science Bob—How to Make Slime

http://sciencebob.com/make-some-starch-slime-today/

Learn about solids and liquids as you make your own substance.

Top 5 Family-Friendly Apps and Websites

Apps

Wonder Bunny Math Race by Fantastec

This app features adorable bunnies, wacky vehicles, and math learning challenges to keep kids challenged and entertained.

Chicktionary by Soap

This fun word game challenges players to unscramble letters to find different words.

Explorium: Ocean for Kids by Applied Systems Ltd.

This adventurous app allows kids to learn amazing facts about the ocean and its inhabitants as well as play fun games.

Websites

ABCya

http://www.abcya.com

This site focuses on a variety of reading and math skills through fun games, puzzles, mazes, and exercises.

Funbrain

http://www.funbrain.com/kidscenter.html

Fun, arcade-style games covering a variety of concepts at all grade levels make this a great website for busy families.

Top 5 Games to Play in the Car

Find 100

Choose an item that is likely to be seen during your car ride or road trip. Then, have your child count how many times he or she sees the item. Once your child reaches 100, give him or her another item to find.

Create a Story

Create a story one sentence at a time. Start off by creating an opening sentence of a story. You might say, "Once upon a time, there was a small village of talking chickens." The next player must continue the story by adding on the next sentence.

Add It Up License Plates

Call out the numbers on a license plate and see who can add two of the numbers up the fastest! For example, if the license plate number reads 1ABC234, players might add 1 + 2. The person who is the first to answer correctly gets a point. The first person to reach 10 points wins! The total can be varied depending on the length of the car ride.

Animal Name Game

Say the name of an animal out loud. Then, the next player has to think of an animal that begins with the last letter of the previous animal name. For example, one person might say turtle. The next player might say eagle. Make sure to point out the ending letters of the words and to sound out the letters to support your child. Be careful and creative when thinking about the animal name—no repeats are allowed!

Car Ride Scavenger Hunt

Make a list of various items you might see on a car ride or road trip. The items can be adjusted according to the scenery. For example, you could list rural items such as a cow, a farmhouse, or an empty field. Or you can list urban items such as a skyscraper, a mailbox, or a phone booth. If possible, include pictures of the items on the list to provide additional support for your child. Have your child try to find each item from the list.

Top 5 Books to Read Aloud

A Lion in Paris by Beatrice Alemagna

This book tells the story of a lion who moves to Paris seeking excitement, but instead finds that he feels lonely in a new city and must find his own identity. The large size and the beautiful illustrations make it perfect for lap reading or story time.

Frog and Toad are Friends by Arnold Lobel

This Caldecott Honor book follows two best friends, Frog and Toad. The book is filled with five stories of the duo's interesting escapades and adventures. Each story is just short enough to make it perfect for a quick bedtime story or a short read-aloud for your child to practice his or her reading skills.

The Day the Crayons Quit by Drew Daywalt

What would happen if all the crayons in your child's crayon box decided to quit? Your child will love the imaginative use of letters to explain each crayon's reasons for quitting. The unique and humorous illustrations help bring each letter to life.

Miss Nelson is Missing! by James Marshall

When sweet Miss Nelson goes missing, the misbehaving kids in Room 207 get a new, foul-tempered substitute teacher to set them straight. Your child will love the humorous story as well as the detailed illustrations.

The Book with No Pictures by B.J. Novak

Simple yet imaginative, this humorous book is filled only with words in various fonts and bright colors. Perfect for reading aloud, each page of this book prompts the reader to exclaim funny noises, silly words, and laughable sentences. The lightheartedness of this book will make your child laugh while introducing him or her to the idea that the written word can be fun and enjoyable.

Week 1

This week, let's blast through summer learning loss by:

- ◆ saying rhyming words

- ◆ responding to a text about the beach

- ◆ writing a letter about wanting a pet

- ◆ drawing a symmetrical leaf

- ◆ filling jars with dots

- ◆ counting cars and dogs

- ◆ solving a problem about pies

- ◆ connecting dots

- ◆ playing a math game

Rhyme Time

Directions: Name the picture in each box. Circle the picture that rhymes.

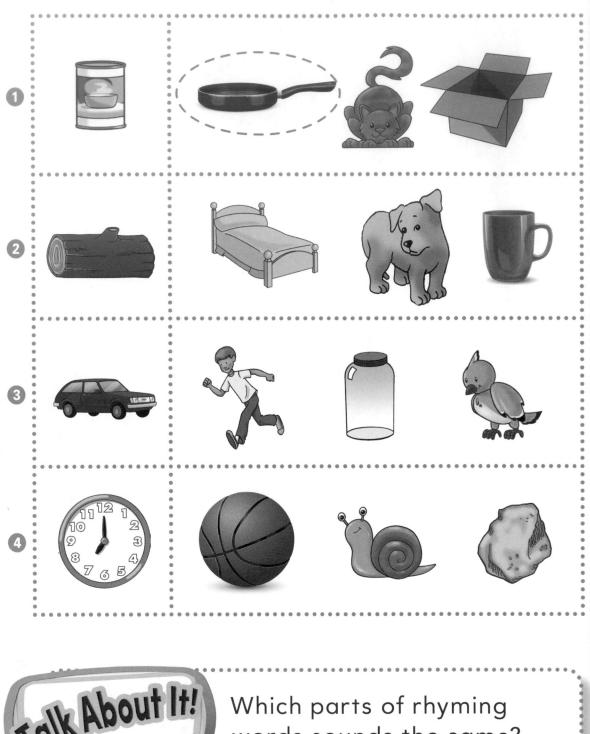

Talk About It!

Which parts of rhyming words sounds the same?

#51551—Summer Blast

Beach Day

Directions: Read the text. Then, answer the questions below.

Sammy and I race to find seashells. We look in the sand and sea. I spot a shell on the shore. I run! Sammy does, too. We giggle as we play tug-of-war in the waves.

❶ Which question helps you learn what a shore is?

Ⓐ Who is in this story?

Ⓑ What is a shore?

Ⓒ What does spot mean?

❷ Who is Sammy?

Ⓐ a dog

Ⓑ a cat

Ⓒ a child

Please, Pretty Please?

Directions: Draw a pet you would like to have. Write a letter about why you should get a pet.

Dear _____,

_____

_____

_____

Love,

_____

The Shape of a Leaf

Directions: Follow the steps to draw a symmetrical leaf.

Steps

① Find a leaf.

② Cut it in half.

③ Tape one half below.

④ Draw the other half so it looks the same.

⑤ Color the half you drew.

Fill a Jar

Directions: Draw dots to fill the jar.

1 Fill the jar with 9 dots.

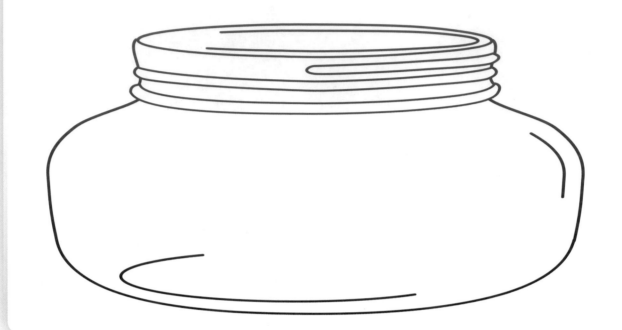

2 Fill the jar with 20 dots.

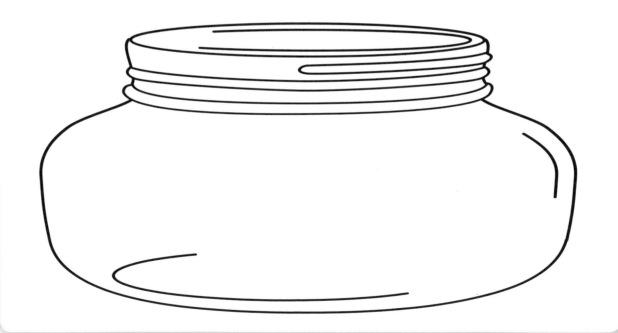

#51551—Summer Blast

Sort and Count by Size

Directions: Answer the questions.

1 Count the little cars. How many? _____

2 Count the big cars. How many? _____

3 Count the big dogs. How many? _____

4 Count the little dogs. How many? _____

Pie Problem

Angela helped her mom make pies for the fair. They made 7 apple pies and 3 cherry pies. How many pies did they make for the fair?

Show It: Draw a picture showing the problem.

Solve It: Write a number sentence.

Explain It: Explain how you solved the problem.

The Surprise

Directions: Connect the dots in order. Then, color the picture.

Talk About It! How do you know which number comes next?

What's My Number?

Number of Players
2

Materials

10 small items to use as counters (pennies, cereal, marshmallows)

Directions

1. Choose a number between 5 and 10. Lay that many items on the table.

2. Player 1 closes his or her eyes. Player 2 picks up some of the items and hides them in his or her hand.

3. Player 1 opens his or her eyes. He or she figures out how many items are hidden based on the number of items still on the table.

4. Switch roles and play again. Change the number of items.

Challenge: Write a number sentence for each problem you solve.

Week 2

This week, let's blast through summer learning loss by:

◆ matching vowel sounds

◆ responding to a text about camping

◆ ordering steps for making a root beer float

◆ designing a stamp

◆ adding shapes

◆ counting sides

◆ solving a problem about juice

◆ matching favorite animals

◆ playing with memories

Choose the Vowel

Directions: Name each picture. Circle the letter that matches the vowel sound.

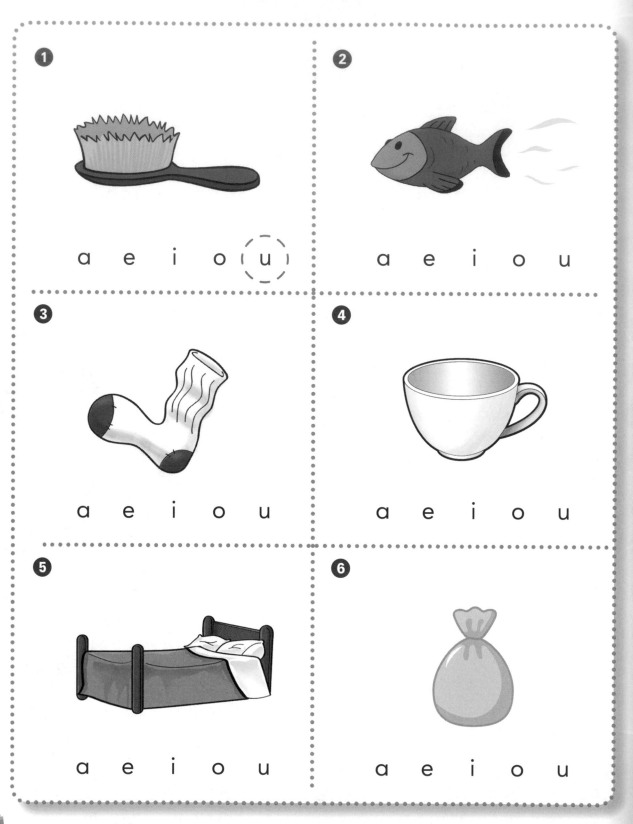

1 a e i o (u)

2 a e i o u

3 a e i o u

4 a e i o u

5 a e i o u

6 a e i o u

#51551—Summer Blast

Camping

Directions: Read the text. Then, answer the questions below.

Sam and Pam love to camp at the beach. They swim. Dad makes a campfire. They fix hot dogs. Yum!

1 Who makes the campfire?

Ⓐ Sam

Ⓑ Pam

Ⓒ Dad

2 How do the hot dogs taste?

Ⓐ bad

Ⓑ okay

Ⓒ very good

Yum, Yum!

Directions: Draw a root beer float. Then, write numbers (1–4) to show the order of the steps to make it.

_____ Enjoy!

_____ Scoop ice cream into a glass.

_____ Gather root beer, ice cream, a glass, and a scooper.

_____ Pour root beer over the ice cream.

Stamp Art

Directions: Draw a stamp showing an American symbol.

Add These Shapes

Directions: Make addition problems with the shapes. Write the total.

Counting Sides

Directions: Count the sides. Write how many.

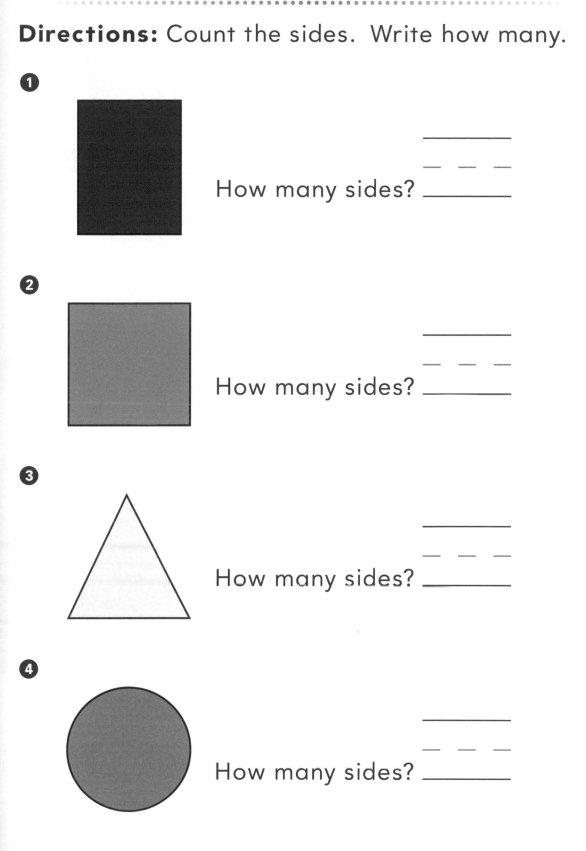

1 How many sides? _____

2 How many sides? _____

3 How many sides? _____

4 How many sides? _____

Juice to Go

William and his sister Jane were playing at home. Their friends Ty and Lynne came over to play. All the kids wanted juice boxes. How many juice boxes do they need?

Show It: Draw a picture showing the problem.

Solve It: Write a number sentence.

Explain It: Explain how you solved the problem.

Favorite Animals

Directions: Read the clues. Draw lines to connect the children to their favorite animals.

> Ron's favorite animal can fly.
>
> Lin's favorite animal lives in water.
>
> Ted's favorite animal does not have legs.

Ron

snake

Lin

eagle

Ted

dolphin

Here I Grow!

Number of Players
2–6

Materials

◆ *Timeline* (page 103)

◆ photos of you as a baby, toddler, and now

Directions

1 Look at photos of you as a baby, a toddler, and now.

2 Name children you know who are babies and toddlers.

3 Discuss what babies and toddlers can do and cannot do.

4 Draw pictures of something you could do at each age on the *Timeline* on page 103.

5 Talk about how other things grow and change (for example, plants and animals).

Week 3

This week, let's blast through summer learning loss by:

- capitalizing words

- learning about Abraham Lincoln

- writing about spending money

- drawing cloud shapes

- finding greater than or less than

- comparing objects

- solving a problem about apple picking

- going through a maze

- playing a matching game

Capital Mistake

Directions: Put check marks by sentences that are correct.

1 I have a dog. ☑

i have a dog. ☐

2 My dog has spots. ☐

my dog has spots. ☐

3 May i pet your dog? ☐

May I pet your dog? ☐

4 your dog is big! ☐

Your dog is big! ☐

Honest Abe

Directions: Read the text. Then, answer the questions below.

Abe Lincoln was our president. He did a good job. He worked hard. Lincoln was a good man. He told the truth. People called him Honest Abe.

It is good to tell the truth. We love Honest Abe!

❶ What does **honest** mean?

Ⓐ sleepy

Ⓑ truthful

Ⓒ fast

❷ Which does **not** tell us Abe was honest?

Ⓐ It is good to tell the truth.

Ⓑ People called him Honest Abe.

Ⓒ He told the truth.

Spending Money!

Directions: Imagine you had $20. Draw and write about what you would do with the money.

#51551—Summer Blast

Cloudy Weather

Directions: Sometimes people see shapes in clouds. Draw a cloud in the shape of an object or an animal.

More and Less

Directions: Complete the steps.

① Circle the group that is less.

② Circle the group that is greater.

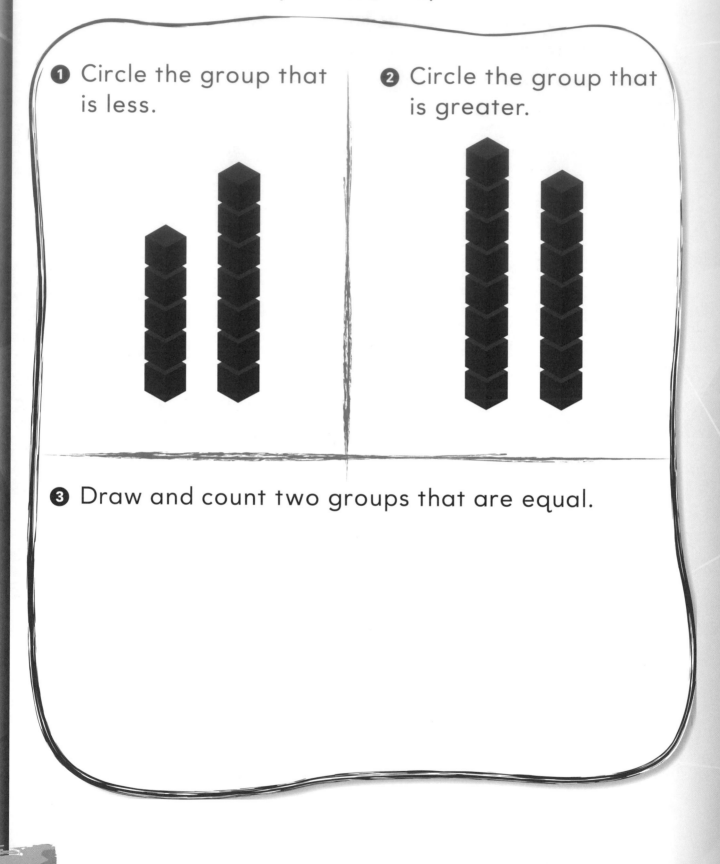

③ Draw and count two groups that are equal.

#51551—Summer Blast

Light as a Feather

Directions: Circle the lighter object in each box.

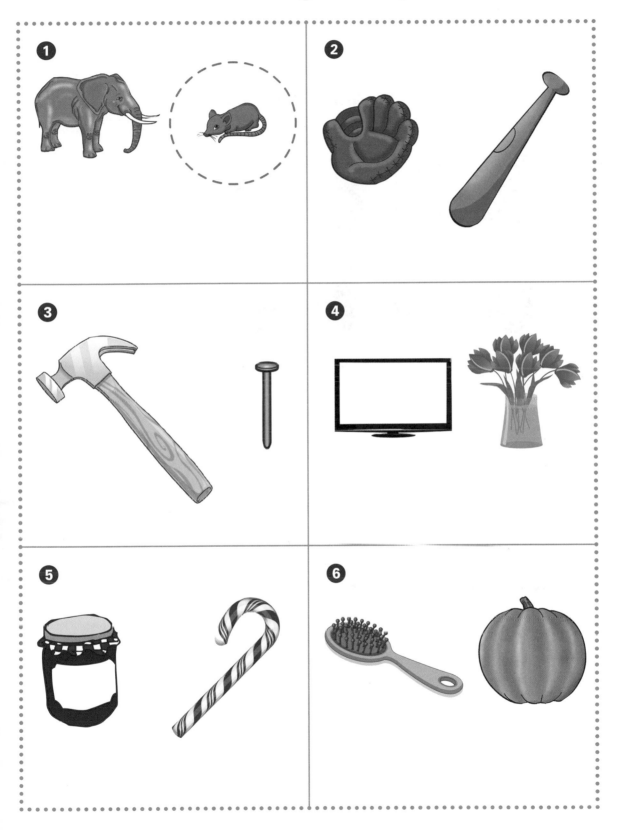

Apple Picking

Steven helped his sister pick 10 apples from their apple tree. Steven ate 3 of them. How many apples did Steven's sister have left?

Show It: Draw a picture showing the problem.

Solve It: Write a number sentence.

Explain It: Explain how you solved the problem.

#51551—Summer Blast

Find the Flag

Directions: Help the soldier find his way to the flag.

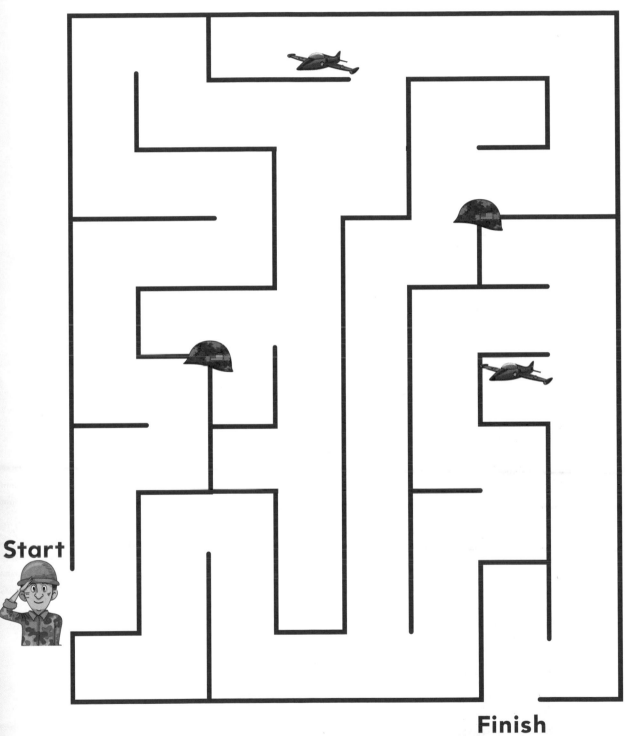

Start

Finish

American Symbols Match

Number of Players
2

Materials

◆ *American Symbols Cards* (pages 105 and 107)

Directions

❶ Cut apart the *American Symbols Cards* on pages 105 and 107.

❷ Shuffle the cards and place them facedown into two rows of five cards.

❹ One player turns over two cards. If the picture matches the American symbol, keep the card pair. If the cards do not match, turn them back over. Remember where they are so you can make a match next time.

❺ Take turns flipping over pairs of cards until all the cards have been matched.

#51551—Summer Blast

Week 4

This week, let's blast through summer learning loss by:

- changing words

- responding to a text about wolves

- writing about and drawing your favorite stuffed animal

- designing a shield

- counting balls

- categorizing buttons

- solving a problem about crackers

- solving a crossword

- playing a math game

New Words

Directions: Change one letter. Write the new word.

1 mom	mop
2 hat	
3 cap	
4 map	

The Mix-Up

Directions: Read the text. Then, answer the questions below.

The Big Bad Wolf met Wolf in the forest.

"Where are you going?" asked Wolf.

"To see Grandma," said the Big Bad Wolf.

"No! You go to the pigs!" cried Wolf.

"Oh, I forgot! Sorry," said the Big Bad Wolf.

And away they went.

1 How are Wolf and Big Bad Wolf the same?

Ⓐ They are going to see someone.

Ⓑ They are going to see the pigs.

Ⓒ They are going to see Grandma.

2 How are Wolf and Big Bad Wolf different?

Ⓐ They are in the forest.

Ⓑ They are not nice.

Ⓒ Big Bad Wolf is going to see the pigs. Wolf is not.

Favorite Stuffy

Directions: Draw and write about your favorite stuffed animal or toy.

#51551—Summer Blast

Famous Person Shield

Directions: Think of a famous person you have learned about. Add designs to the shield for that person.

Count All of Those Balls!

Directions: Count the balls. Then, follow the steps.

1   How many? _____

Draw 4 more. How many now? _____

2   How many? _____

Draw 5 more. How many now? _____

3   How many? _____

Draw 2 more. How many now? _____

Buttons, Buttons

Directions: The first circle shows buttons with an attribute. In the second circle, draw buttons that are not like the first group.

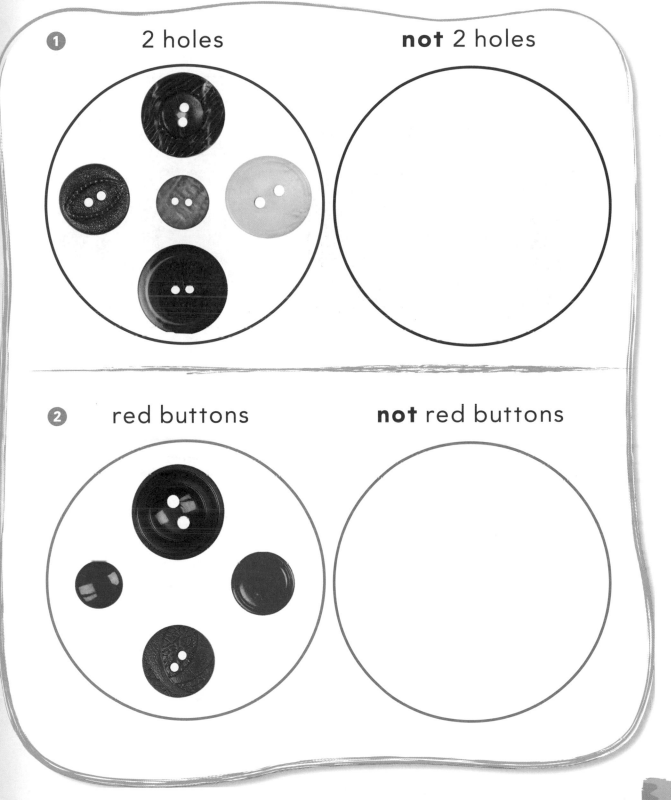

1   2 holes   **not** 2 holes

2   red buttons   **not** red buttons

A Tray of Crackers

Erin and her brother James asked their dad for a snack. He put 12 crackers on a tray for Erin. He put crackers on a plate for James. How will the kids know they get an equal number of crackers?

Show It: Draw a picture showing the problem.

Solve It: Write a number sentence.

Explain It: Explain how you solved the problem.

#51551—Summer Blast

Number Crossword

Directions: Solve the clues. Complete the crossword puzzle using the Answer Box.

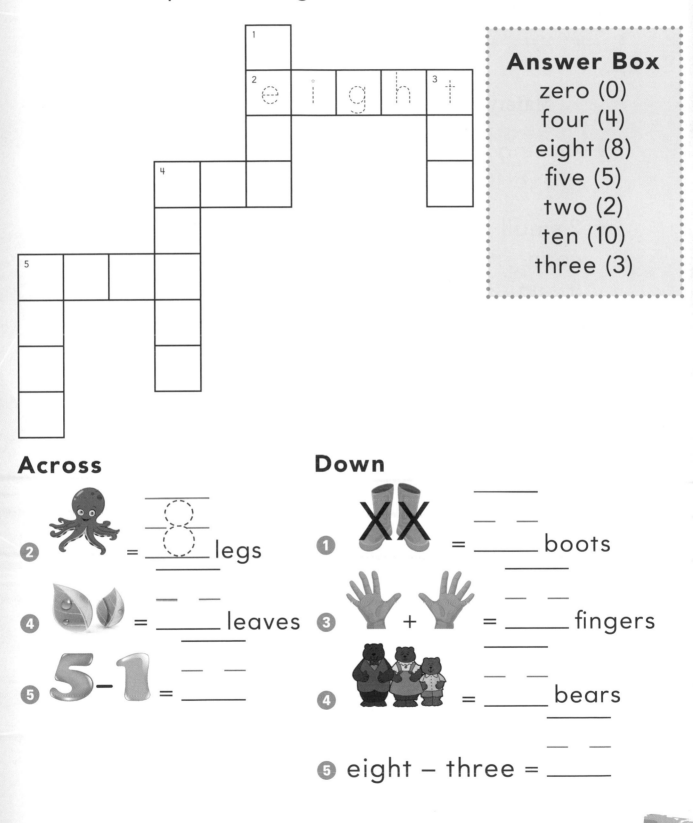

Answer Box
zero (0)
four (4)
eight (8)
five (5)
two (2)
ten (10)
three (3)

Across

2. = _____ legs

4. = _____ leaves

5. 5 - 1 = _____

Down

1. = _____ boots

3. + = _____ fingers

4. = _____ bears

5. eight – three = _____

Add Them Up

Number of Players
2

Materials

◆ *Adding Mat* (page 109)

◆ 2 small counters (pennies, cereal, marshmallows)

◆ paper

◆ pencil

Directions

1 One player places a counter on a box from the *Adding Mat* on page 109.

2 The other player places a counter on a different box from the mat.

3 Add the numbers in the marked boxes together.

4 Remove the counters and play again.

5 Continue placing counters and adding up the numbers until all of the numbers are used.

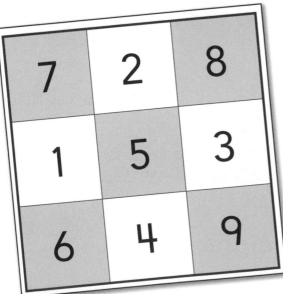

Week 5

This week, let's blast through summer learning loss by:

- completing sentences

- responding to a text about frogs

- drawing and writing about a funny event

- designing a creature

- counting bears

- hunting for shapes

- solving a problem about bugs

- thinking about the weather

- playing a shadow guessing game

Find the Right Word

Directions: Choose a word from the Word Bank to complete each sentence.

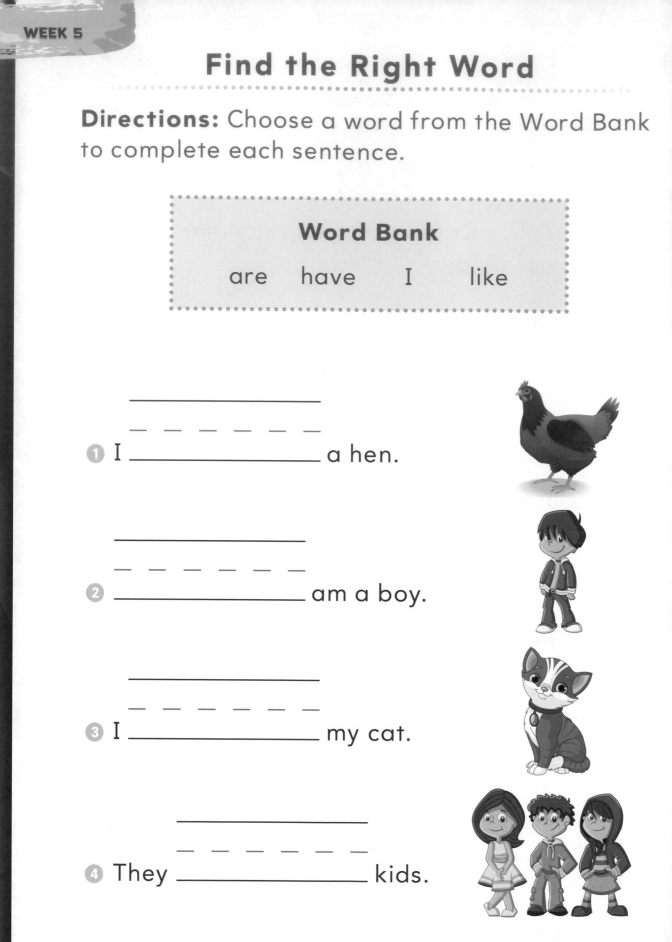

Word Bank

are   have   I   like

1 I _____ a hen.

2 _____ am a boy.

3 I _____ my cat.

4 They _____ kids.

#51551—Summer Blast

Frogs Are Neat

Directions: Read the text. Then, answer the questions below.

A baby frog is called a tadpole. It starts as an egg. It has to stay in water. A tadpole uses its tail to move. It has very tiny teeth. It finds food in the water. The tadpole takes more than 12 weeks to grow up.

① What is a baby frog called?

② Where does it live?

③ How does it move?

④ Where does it find food?

That Was Funny!

Directions: Draw and write about the funniest thing you have ever seen.

Design a New Animal

Directions: Design a new animal by combining parts of other animals. Your animal could have the fin of a dolphin, the neck of a giraffe, and the legs of a cheetah. Use your imagination!

Count the Bears

Directions: Count the bears. First, count by ones. Then, count by tens.

① How many bears?

_____

− − − −

_____

② How many bears?

_____

− − − −

_____

③ How many bears?

_____

− − − −

_____

Try this! How many bears on this page?

_____

− − − −

There are _____ bears on this page.

Shape Hunt

Directions: Find an example in your house of each shape. Draw a picture of what you find.

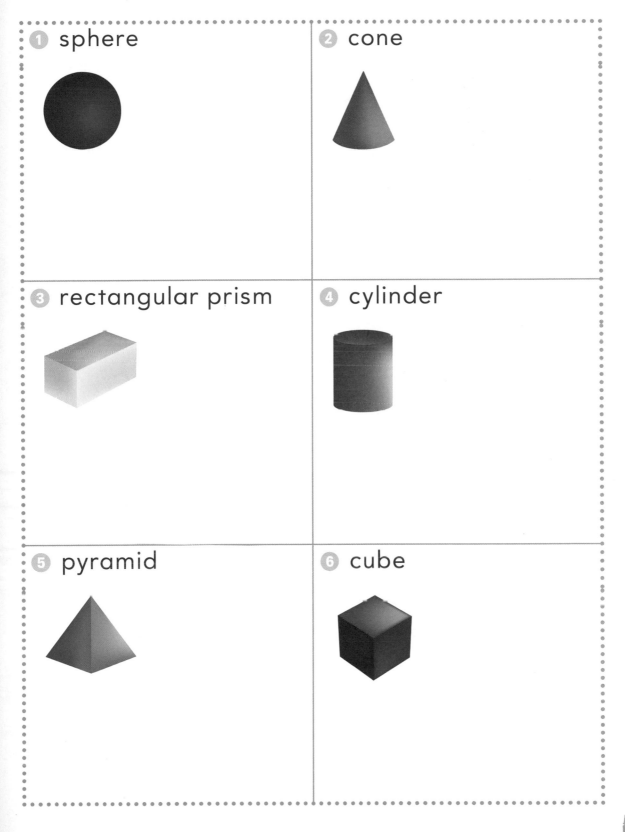

① sphere

② cone

③ rectangular prism

④ cylinder

⑤ pyramid

⑥ cube

Big Problems with Bugs!

Directions: Count the bugs in each group. Write the numbers. Then, add the bugs.

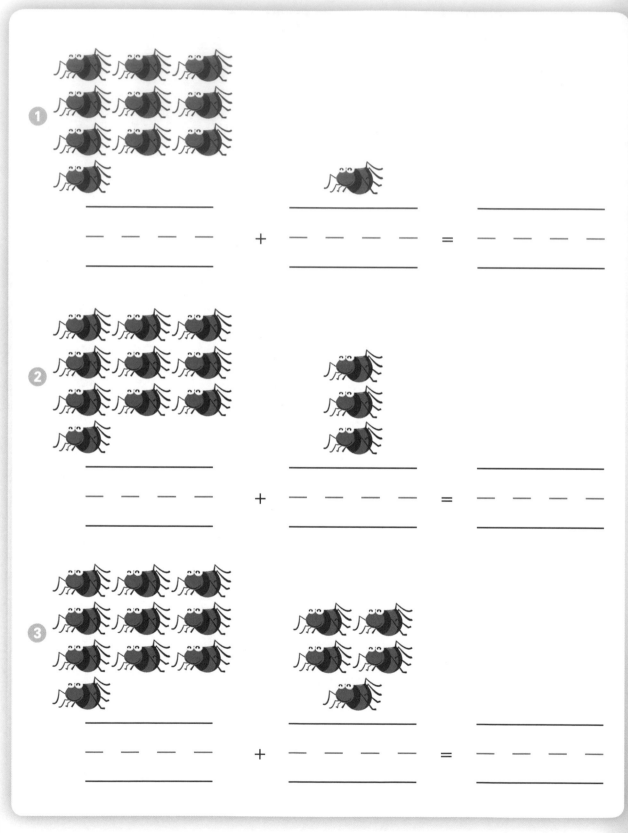

#51551—Summer Blast

Weather Sudoku

Directions: Follow the steps.

Every mini grid must have each weather picture.
Every row must have each weather picture.
Every column must have each weather picture.

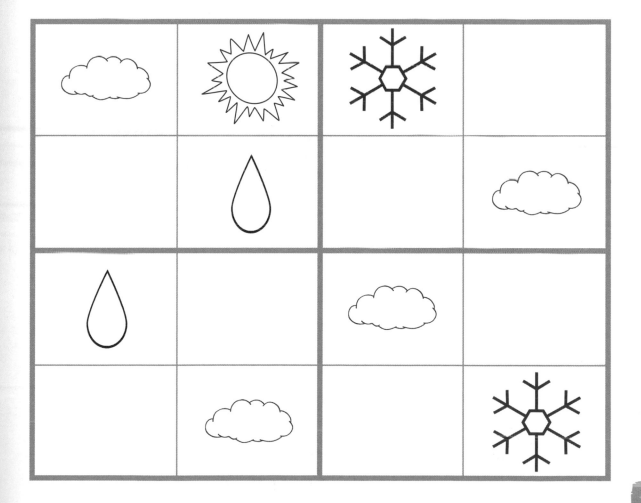

In the Dark

Number of Players
2–6

Materials

◆ flashlight

◆ a variety of toys or stuffed animals

Directions

1. Look at all the toys or stuffed animals you have gathered.

2. Turn the lights out in the room.

3. Turn on the flashlight and shine it against a wall.

4. Take turns holding one of the objects between the flashlight and the wall causing shadows to be cast on the wall. **Note:** Make sure the toy is hidden from players guessing.

5. Other players guess which toy or stuffed animal it is by looking at the shadow.

6. Talk about which toys or stuffed animals were easier and harder to identify and why.

Week 6

This week, let's blast through summer learning loss by:

◆ picture spelling

◆ responding to a text about a birthday

◆ writing dialogue

◆ designing a pirate map

◆ problem solving for leftovers

◆ finding lengths of snakes

◆ solving a problem about fruit

◆ searching for words

◆ playing a destination game

Spelling Fun

Directions: Name each picture. Spell each picture.

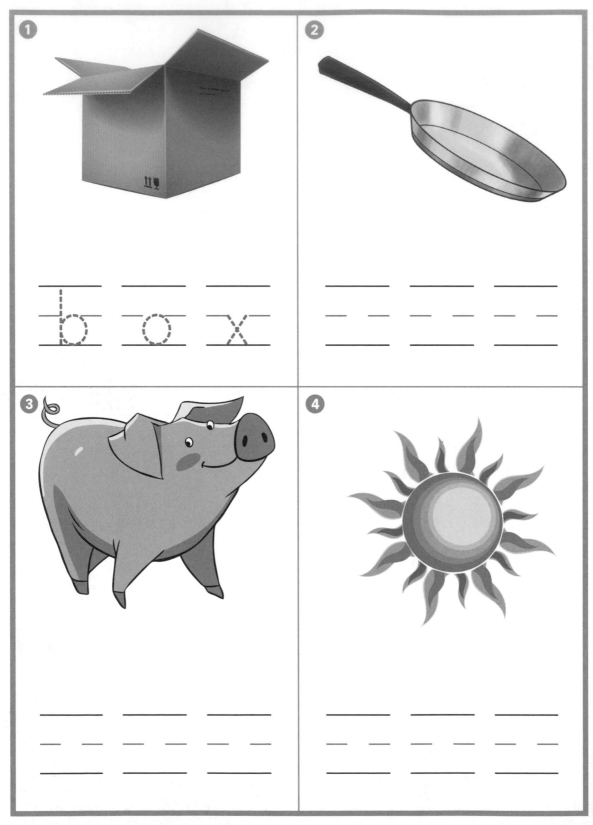

1. b o x

2. _ _ _ _ _

3. _ _ _ _ _

4. _ _ _ _ _

Jack's Birthday

Directions: Read the text. Then, answer the questions.

Today is Jack's birthday

He sees a big box in his room. It is covered in brown paper.

Jack opens the box. Wow! There is a bright red boat inside.

He finds a note. It says "Happy Birthday, Jack!"

1. What is the box covered in?

   Ⓐ brown paper

   Ⓑ yellow paper

   Ⓒ red paper

2. What is in the box?

   Ⓐ Jack

   Ⓑ a boat

   Ⓒ brown paper

What Are They Saying?

Directions: Write what the two people are saying in the speech bubbles.

Argh, Matey!

Directions: Use the symbols in the key to design your own pirate map.

Key

✖ – treasure

🌴 – tree

🦈 – shark

⏶ – hill

〜 – ocean

How Many Are Left?

Directions: Read and solve each question.

1 There were 4 dogs. Then, 3 dogs walked away. Draw the problem.

_____

– – – – –

How many are left? _____

2 There were 7 balloons. Then, 2 blew away. Draw the problem.

_____

– – – – –

How many are left? _____

Garden Snakes

Directions: Circle the answers.

1. Which snake is longer? **green** **blue**

2. Which snake is longer? **red** **green**

3. Which snake is the longest? **green** **blue** **red**

4. Order the snakes from longest to shortest. Write the colors of the snakes.

Longest ••••••••••••••••► **Shortest**

  #51551—Summer Blast

How Much Fruit?

Kevin is buying fruit. He buys 12 bananas. He already has 8 apples at home. He wants to have an equal number of bananas and apples. How many apples should he buy?

Show It: Draw a picture showing the problem.

Solve It: Write a number sentence.

Explain It: Explain how you solved the problem.

#51551—Summer Blast

Land and Water Word Search

Directions: Circle the land and water words in the word search.

Land and Water Words

hill	island	river
ocean		mountain

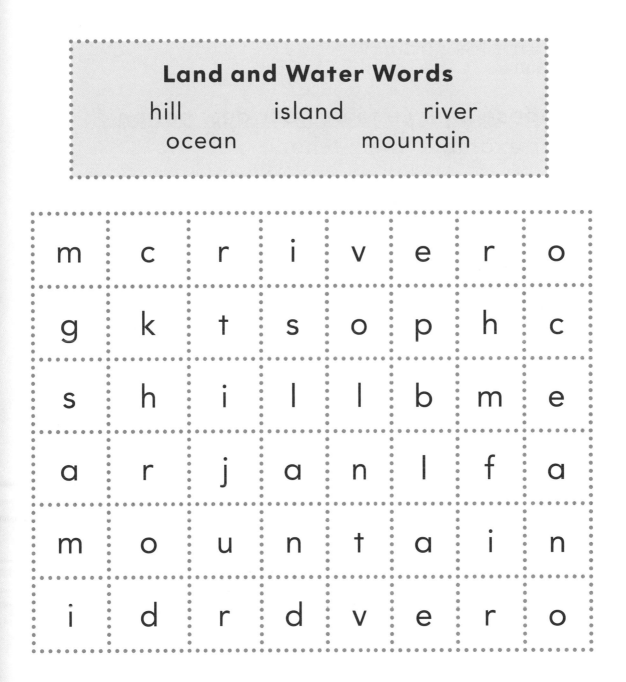

m	c	r	i	v	e	r	o
g	k	t	s	o	p	h	c
s	h	i	l	l	b	m	e
a	r	j	a	n	l	f	a
m	o	u	n	t	a	i	n
i	d	r	d	v	e	r	o

Get Me There

Directions

1 Choose a place to be your destination (for example, the kitchen).

2 Choose who will give directions and who will follow the directions. One player gives the other player directions on how to get to the destination using the directions *forward*, *backward*, *right*, and *left* (for example, "Take 3 steps forward.").

3 Continue giving directions until you get to the destination.

4 Trade places, and choose a new destination.

Week 7

This week, let's blast through summer learning loss by:

- uncovering the complete sentence

- responding to a text about American symbols

- writing about your special day

- drawing something new

- counting shapes

- adding up shoes

- telling a math story

- finding the next number

- playing a tic-tac-toe game

Sentence Detective

Directions: Write **yes** by the complete sentences. Write **no** by the phrases.

1. _____ in the dog house

2. _____ Spot has some bones.

3. _____ a hole under the big tree

4. _____ When you are

5. _____ It's great!

National Symbols

Directions: Read the text. Then, answer the questions below.

The United States has many symbols. The flag has 13 stripes and 50 stars. The Statue of Liberty and the Liberty Bell are symbols of freedom. The bald eagle is a strong bird. It is a symbol of strength.

1 Which is a symbol of strength?

Ⓐ the flag

Ⓑ the Liberty Bell

Ⓒ the bald eagle

2 Which is **not** a symbol of freedom?

Ⓐ stars

Ⓑ the Liberty Bell

Ⓒ the Statue of Liberty

A Special Day

Directions: Imagine you are an adult for a day. Draw and write about what you would do or where you would go.

#51551—Summer Blast

What Is It?

Directions: Use the apple outline to draw a picture of something other than an apple.

Shape Count

Directions: Count the sets of objects in each row. Draw a line to match the number on the animal.

#51551—Summer Blast

So Many Shoes!

Directions: Count the shoes in each category. Write the numbers.

1

_____

_____

_____

2

_____

_____

_____

Make a Story

Directions: Make up an addition or a subtraction story using the drawings.

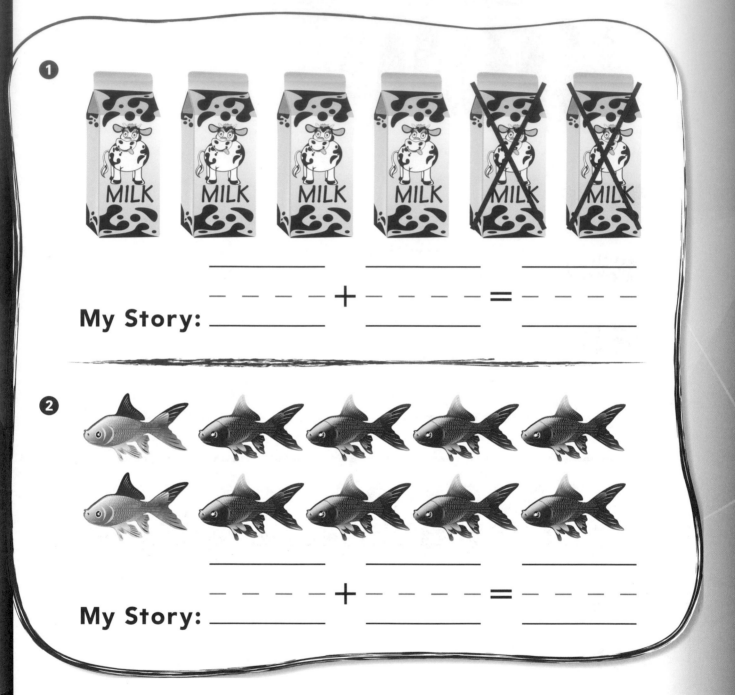

1

_____ _____ _____
– – – – + – – – – = – – – –

My Story: _____ _____ _____

2

_____ _____ _____
– – – – + – – – – = – – – –

My Story: _____ _____ _____

Try this! Make your own addition and subtraction story using the numbers 2, 3, and 5.

Next Number

Directions: For each circle number, find a triangle number that comes next. Color both shapes the same color.

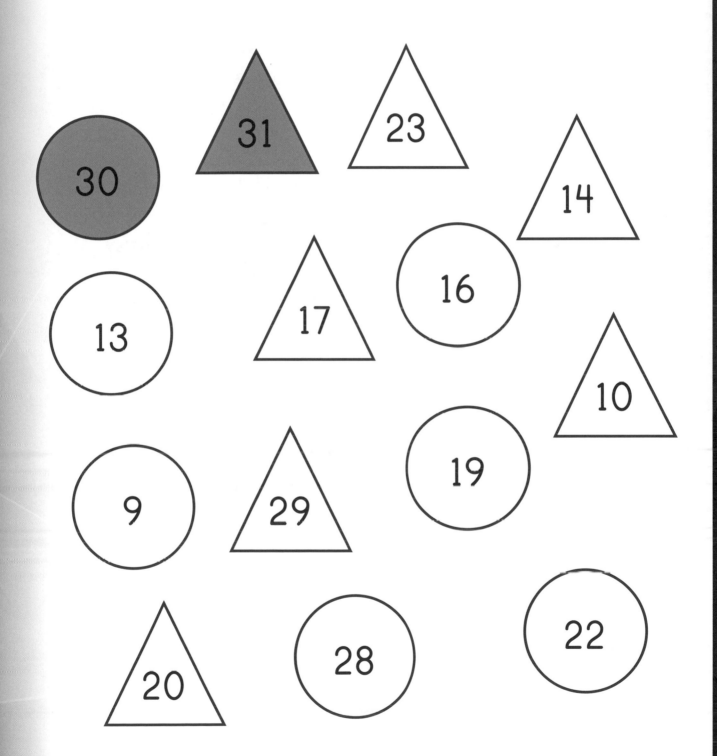

 #51551—Summer Blast

Tic-Tac-4

Number of Players
2

Materials

- *Tic-Tac-4 Game Board* (page 111)

- *Tic-Tac-4 Game Cards* (pages 113 and 115)

- 2 sets of differently colored or shaped counters (cereal, pieces of paper, etc.)

Directions

❶ Place the *Tic-Tac-4 Game Board* on page 111 in the center of the table.

❷ Cut apart the *Tic-Tac-4 Game Cards* on pages 113 and 115. Shuffle them, and place them facedown in a pile.

❸ The first player turns over a card and puts a counter on a space of the game board that matches the card.

❹ Repeat with the second player.

❺ The first player to have counters on 4 spaces in a row in any direction is the winner.

Week 8

This week, let's blast through summer learning loss by:

- figuring out plural words

- responding to a text about a dog

- drawing and writing about the joys of fishing

- designing your own community

- adding to make ten

- comparing shapes

- making and breaking 7

- revealing the riddle

- playing a sound game

More Than One?

Directions: Circle the right words for the problem.

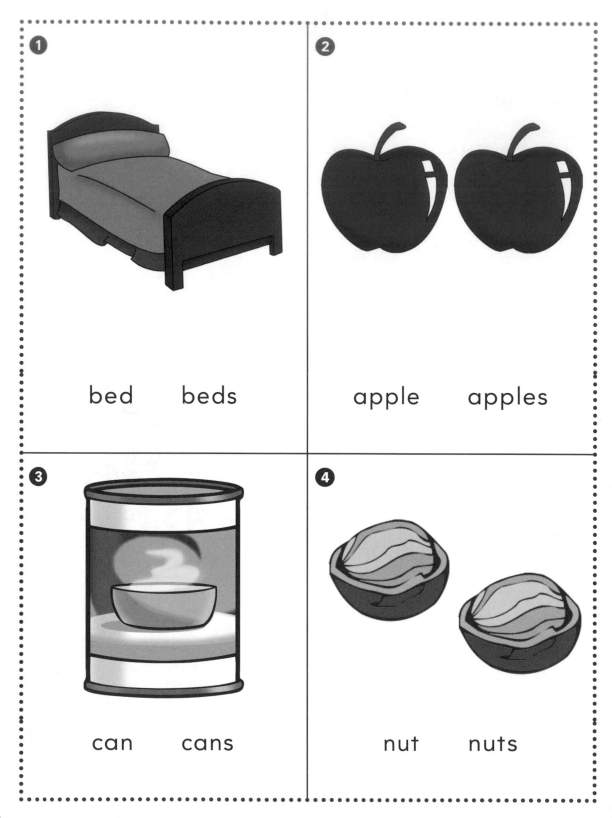

1

bed   beds

2

apple   apples

3

can   cans

4

nut   nuts

#51551—Summer Blast

Pal the Dog

Directions: Read the text. Then, answer the questions.

Pal is a dog. Pal can open the door. He can get Tim's shoes. He helps Tim a lot. He is a good friend.

1 What kind of animal is Pal?

_____

_ _ _ _ _ _ _ _ _ _ _ _ _ _ _

_____

2 What does Pal open?

_____

_ _ _ _ _ _ _ _ _ _ _ _ _ _ _

_____

3 What does Pal get?

_____

_ _ _ _ _ _ _ _ _ _ _ _ _ _ _

_____

4 Why is Pal a good friend?

_____

_ _ _ _ _ _ _ _ _ _ _ _ _ _ _

_____

_ _ _ _ _ _ _ _ _ _ _ _ _ _ _

_____

Gone Fishing?

Directions: Draw and write why you would or would not like to go fishing.

My Community

Directions: Use the space below to design your own community. Include the places you would want to visit (for example, the park or the donut shop).

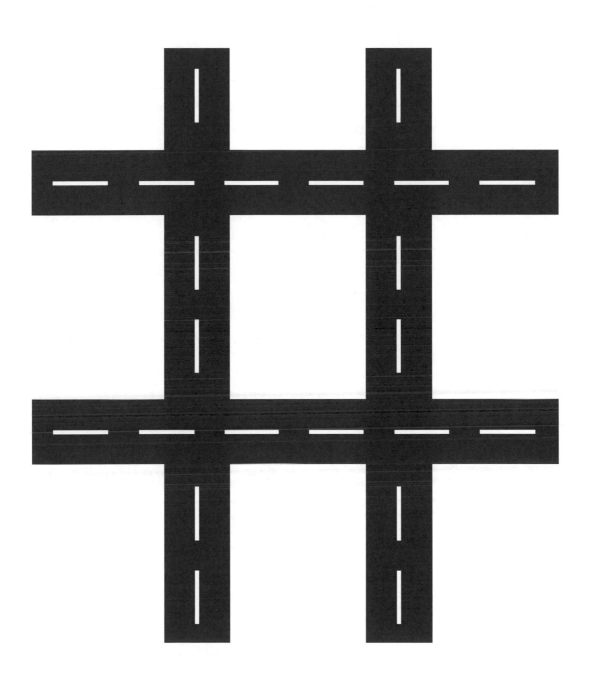

Make Ten

Directions: Solve.

❶ Color 3 circles red. How many yellow circles do you need to make 10?

○ ○ ○ ○ ○
○ ○ ○ ○ ○   _____ + _____ = _____

❷ Color 5 circles red. How many yellow circles do you need to make 10?

○ ○ ○ ○ ○
○ ○ ○ ○ ○   _____ + _____ = _____

❸ Color 2 circles red. How many yellow circles do you need to make 10?

○ ○ ○ ○ ○
○ ○ ○ ○ ○   _____ + _____ = _____

Find the Shapes

Directions: Mark the shapes.

❶ Circle the triangles.

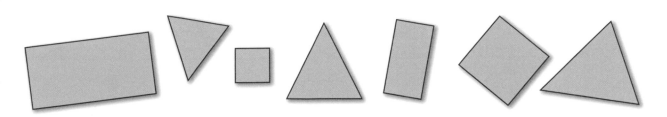

❷ Circle the squares.

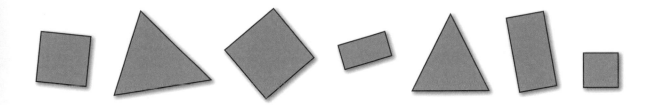

❸ Underline the circles.

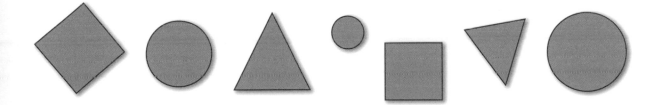

❹ Underline the rectangles.

Make or Break

Directions: Make and break the number 7.

Make It!	Break It!
3 and 4 make 7.	7 is 2 and 5.
_____ and _____ make 7.	7 is _____ and _____.
_____ and _____ make 7.	7 is _____ and _____.
_____ and _____ make 7.	7 is _____ and _____.

#51551—*Summer Blast*

Riddle Me This

Directions: Use the code to find the answer to the riddle.

Code

| a | b | i | n | o | r | w |

What bow can't be tied?

Draw a picture of the answer.

Hear This!

Number of Players
2–6

Directions

❶ Choose a player to go first. The other players close their eyes.

❷ The first player makes a noise in the room such as turning on the water at the sink or getting ice from the freezer.

❸ The other players try to guess what the sound is.

❹ Continue playing by having another player choose a sound to make while the others guess.

❺ Talk about the sounds that were the easiest and the hardest to guess.

Week 9

This week, let's blast through summer learning loss by:

- saying rhyming words

- responding to a text about plants

- making three wishes

- designing a country flag

- subtracting frog hops

- comparing tall and short

- solving math problems

- completing a number puzzle

- playing job charades

Vowel Focus

#51551—Summer Blast

Directions: Circle the words that rhyme with each object.

①		lake rake tap take
②		zone hog cone lone
③	**5**	tip dive alive hive
④		fame can same tame
⑤		hire wire tip tire

#51551—Summer Blast

A Powerful Plant

Directions: Read the text. Then, answer the questions below.

Most plants make their own food. The Venus flytrap is different. This plant eats. It eats insects! It looks as if it has a wide mouth at the ends of its leaves. When an insect crawls onto the leaf, it touches tiny hairs. The tiny hairs pull the insect in to be digested. This makes the "mouth" close tightly. The insect is trapped!

❶ What do the tiny hairs on the leaves do to the insect?

Ⓐ They let the insect go.

Ⓑ They pull the insect in to be digested.

Ⓒ They comfort the insect.

Ⓓ They eat the insect.

❷ What does the Venus flytrap eat?

Ⓐ insects

Ⓑ water

Ⓒ soil

Ⓓ leaves

Three Wishes

Directions: Draw and write about what you would wish for if you had three wishes.

© Shell Education

Flag Art

Directions: Draw a shape. Decorate the shape like the United States flag or the flag of your family's home country.

Hop Backward

Directions: Follow the frog as he hops along the number line.

① What number does the frog hop to? 6 – 3 = _____

② What number does the frog hop to? 6 – 2 = _____

③ What number does the frog hop to? 6 – 4 = _____

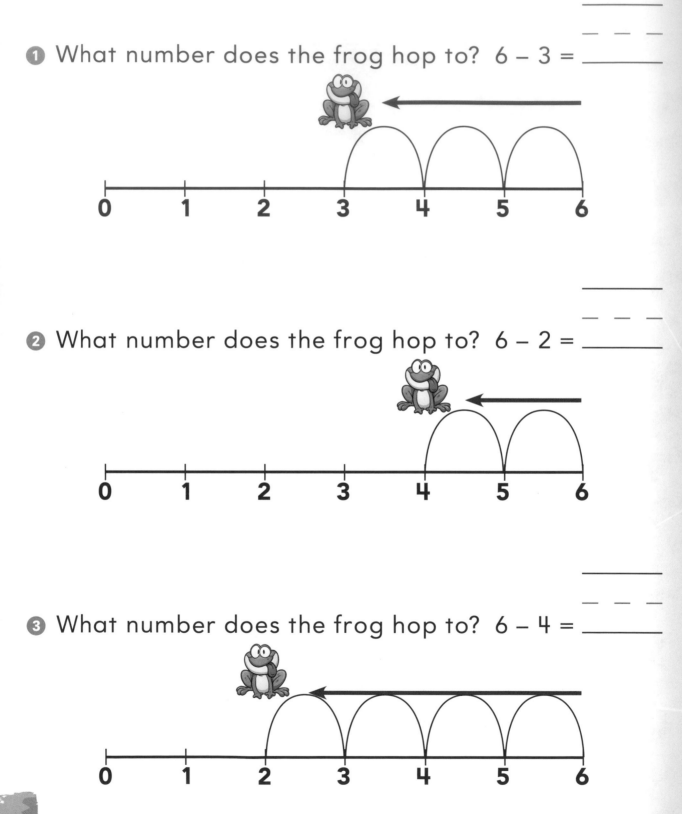

#51551—Summer Blast

Taller and Shorter

Directions: Find things that are taller than and shorter than the objects. Then, answer the questions.

	Taller	Shorter
door		
kitchen counter		
a stuffed animal		
you		

What is the tallest object on your chart?

_____

_ _ _ _ _ _ _ _ _ _ _ _ _

_____

What is the shortest object on your chart?

_____

_ _ _ _ _ _ _ _ _ _ _ _ _

_____

Problems, Problems!

Directions: Solve the problems. Then, circle whether you had to add or subtract.

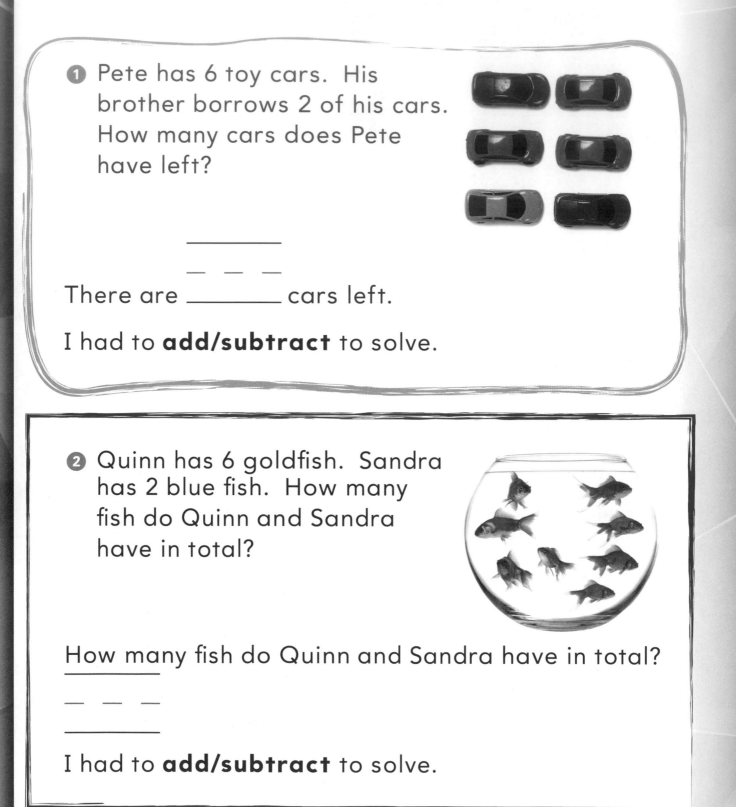

① Pete has 6 toy cars. His brother borrows 2 of his cars. How many cars does Pete have left?

_____

— — —

There are _____ cars left.

I had to **add/subtract** to solve.

② Quinn has 6 goldfish. Sandra has 2 blue fish. How many fish do Quinn and Sandra have in total?

How many fish do Quinn and Sandra have in total?

— — —

_____

I had to **add/subtract** to solve.

#51551—Summer Blast

Number Sudoku

Directions

◆ Every mini grid must have the numbers 1, 2, 3, and 4.

◆ Every column must have the numbers 1, 2, 3, and 4.

◆ Every row must have the numbers 1, 2, 3, and 4.

2			1
	1		
	2	4	
	3		2

Community Jobs Charades

Number of Players
2–6

Materials

◆ *Community Jobs Cards* (page 117)

Mail C...

Vet

Directions

1. Cut apart the *Community Jobs Cards* on page 117.

2. Shuffle the cards and place them facedown in a pile.

3. Have the first player draw a card and secretly look at it. He or she must act out the job.

4. Other players try to guess the job. The person who guesses correctly gets to go next.

5. Try to think of other community jobs that can be acted out once all the cards have been used.

Timeline

Use this timeline with the *Here I Grow!* activity on page 32.

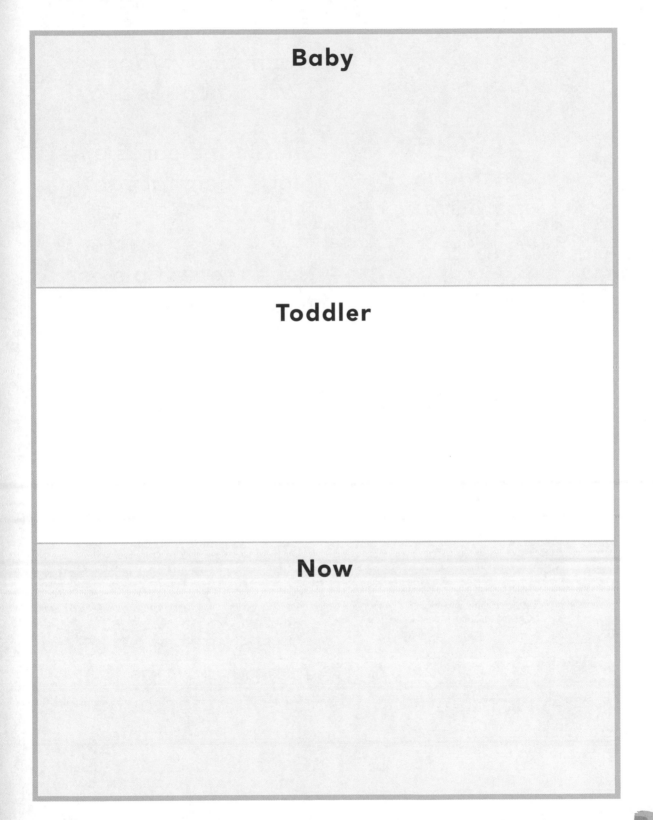

Baby

Toddler

Now

Here I Grow!

American Symbols Cards

Use these cards with the *American Symbols Match* activity on page 42.

bald eagle

Statue of Liberty

American flag

American Symbols Match

American Symbols Match

American Symbols Match

American Symbols Match

American Symbols Match

American Symbols Match

American Symbols Cards (cont.)

Use these cards with the *American Symbols Match* activity on page 42.

	Pledge of Allegiance
	Liberty Bell

American Symbols Match

American Symbols Match

American Symbols Match

American Symbols Match

Adding Mat

Use this mat with the *Add Them Up* activity on page 52.

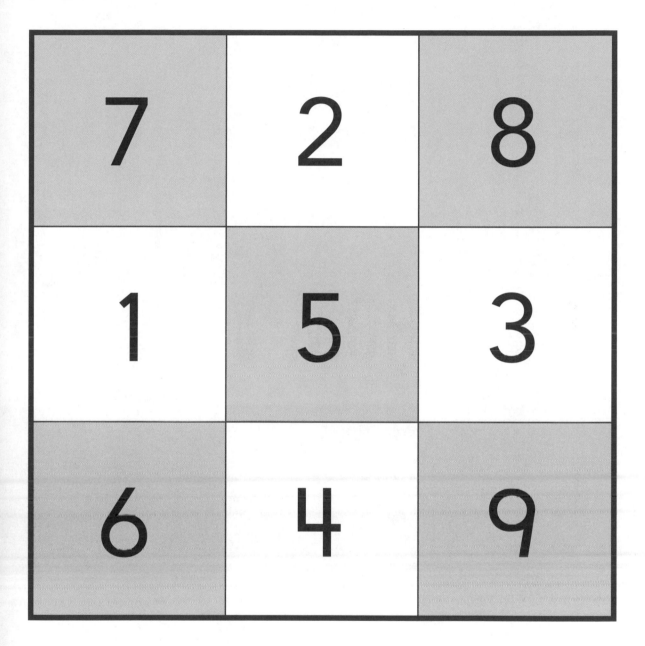

Add Them Up

Tic-Tac-4 Game Board

Use this game board with the *Tic-Tac-4* activity on page 82.

10	17	11	15	19	14
16	12	18	20	11	10
18	16	15	14	19	11
13	19	12	16	12	17
14	13	11	10	17	15
20	18	14	13	20	13

Tic-Tac-4

Tic-Tac-4 Game Cards

Use these cards with the *Tic-Tac-4* activity on page 82.

Tic-Tac-4

Tic-Tac-4

Tic-Tac-4

Tic-Tac-4

Tic-Tac-4

Tic-Tac-4

Tic-Tac-4

Tic-Tac-4

Tic-Tac-4

Tic-Tac-4

Tic-Tac-4

Tic-Tac-4

Tic-Tac-4 Game Cards (cont.)

Use these cards with the *Tic-Tac-4* activity on page 82.

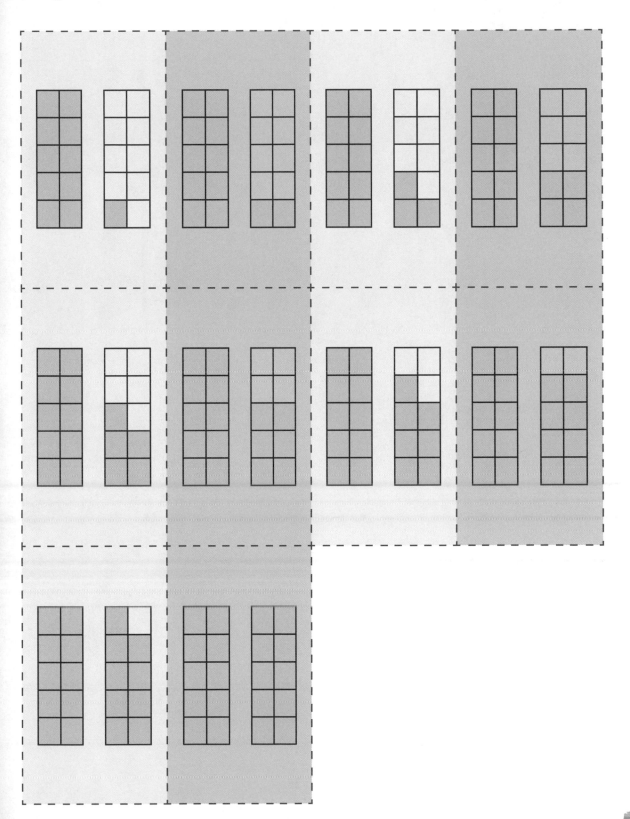

Tic-Tac-4   Tic-Tac-4   Tic-Tac-4   Tic-Tac-4

Tic-Tac-4   Tic-Tac-4   Tic-Tac-4   Tic-Tac-4

Community Jobs Cards (cont.)

Use these cards with the *Community Jobs Charades* activity on page 102.

Police Officer	Mail Carrier	Fire Fighter
Dentist	Doctor	Teacher
Librarian	Bus Driver	Vet

*Community Jobs
Charades*

*Community Jobs
Charades*

*Community Jobs
Charades*

*Community Jobs
Charades*

*Community Jobs
Charades*

*Community Jobs
Charades*

*Community Jobs
Charades*

*Community Jobs
Charades*

*Community Jobs
Charades*

Answer Key

Week 1

Rhyme Time (page 14)

1.  3.
2. 4.

Talk About It: The ends of rhyming words sound the same.

Beach Day (page 15)

1. B   2. C

Please, Pretty Please? (page 16)

Check that the drawing is of a desired pet. The letter should include at least one reason why he or she would like to own the pet.

The Shape of a Leaf (page 17)

Check that the leaf is symmetrical and colored.

Fill a Jar (page 18)

1. 9 dots in the jar
2. 20 dots in the jar

Sort and Count by Size (page 19)

1. 3   3. 5
2. 3   4. 3

Pie Problem (page 20)

Show It: 7 apple pies; 3 cherry pies
Solve It: 10 pies; 7 + 3 = 10
Explain It: Answer should include 7 + 3, for total of 10 pies.

The Surprise (page 21)

Talk About It: Discuss how predictions were made about which number comes next.

What's My Number? (page 22)

Check that the right numbers are guessed.

Week 2

Choose the Vowel (page 24)

1. u   3. o   5. e
2. i   4. u   6. a

Camping (page 25)

1. C   2. C

Yum, Yum! (page 26)

The steps should be numbered in the following way:

1. Gather the ingredients and a glass.
2. Scoop ice cream into a glass.
3. Pour root beer over the ice cream.
4. Enjoy!

Stamp Art (page 27)

Check that the stamp includes an American symbol.

Add These Shapes (page 28)

1. 2 + 6 = 8
2. 3 + 1 = 4
3. 5 + 5 = 10

Counting Sides (page 29)

1. 4   3. 3
2. 4   4. 0

Juice to Go (page 30)

Show It: William, Jane, Ty, and Lynne. How many juice boxes?
Solve It: 4
Explain It: Answers should include adding together all of the children that were playing.

Favorite Animals (page 31)

Ron—eagle
Lin—dolphin
Ted—snake

Here I Grow! (page 32)

Example answers:
baby: crawl
toddler: walk
now: ride a bike

Week 3

Capital Mistake (page 34)

Sentences that should have check marks:

1. **I** have a dog.
2. **My** dog has spots.
3. May **I** pet your dog?
4. **Your** dog is big!

Answer Key (cont.)

Honest Abe (page 35)

1. B   **2.** A

Spending Money! (page 36)

Check that response includes what would be done with $20.

Cloudy Weather (page 37)

Check that the cloud is in the shape of an object or animal.

More and Less (page 38)

1.   **2.**

3. Check that two equal groups are drawn.

Light as a Feather (page 39)

The following images should be circled:

1. mouse   **4.** flowers

2. baseball mitt   **5.** candy cane

3. nail   **6.** brush

Apple Picking (page 40)

Show It: 10 apples; ate 3; how many are left?

Solve It: 10 − 3 = 7; 7 apples

Explain It: Answer should include subtracting 10 − 3 to find the 7 apples left.

Find the Flag (page 41)

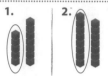

American Symbols Match (page 42)

Check that each picture card is matched to the corresponding American symbol.

Week 4

New Words (page 44)

1. mop   **3.** can

2. cat   **4.** man

The Mix-Up (page 45)

1. A   **2.** C

Favorite Stuffy (page 46)

Check that response is about a favorite stuffed animal or toy.

Famous Person Shield (page 47)

Check that the shield is designed to represent a famous person.

Count All of Those Balls! (page 48)

1. 3; 7   **3.** 5; 7

2. 4; 9

Buttons, Buttons (page 49)

1. Check that drawings of buttons have any number of holes other than two.

2. Check that drawings of buttons are any color other than red.

A Tray of Crackers (page 50)

Show It: Crackers are arranged in the three rows on the tray. They are arranged in two rows on the plate.

Solve It: 12 are on the tray. 12 are on the plate.

Explain It: Answer may include that the kids can count the crackers to find out both the tray and the plate include 12 crackers even though they are arranged differently.

Number Crossword (page 51)

Across	Down
2. 8	**1.** 0
4. 2	**3.** 10
5. 4	**4.** 3
	5. 5

Add Them Up (page 52)

Check that the addition is correct.

Week 5

Find the Right Word (page 54)

1. have   **3.** like

2. I   **4.** are

Frogs Are Neat (page 55)

1. tadpole   **3.** with its tail

2. in water   **4.** in the water

That Was Funny! (page 56)

Check that the response includes a funny thing.

Answer Key (cont.)

Design a New Animal (page 57)

Check that the drawing is of a new animal.

Count the Bears (page 58)

1. 10
3. 30
2. 20

Try This! There are 60 bears on this page.

Shape Hunt (page 59)

Check that items chosen match the given shapes.

Big Problems with Bugs! (page 60)

1. $10 + 1 = 11$
3. $10 + 5 = 15$
2. $10 + 3 = 13$

Weather Sudoku (page 61)

In the Dark (page 62)

If the guesses are incorrect, let the child continue guessing.

Week 6

Spelling Fun (page 64)

1. box
3. pig
2. pan
4. sun

Jack's Birthday (page 65)

1. A
2. B

What Are They Saying? (page 66)

Check that the speech bubbles are filled with dialogue.

Argh, Matey! (page 67)

Check that each symbol is used in the map.

How Many Are Left? (page 68)

1. $4 - 3 = 1$
2. $7 - 2 = 5$

Garden Snakes (page 69)

1. blue
3. blue
2. red
4. blue, red, green

How Much Fruit? (page 70)

Show It: 12 bananas; 8 apples

Solve It: $8 + 4 = 12$ apples

Explain It: Answer should include that Kevin should buy 4 apples to have an equal number of bananas and apples.

Land and Water Word Search (page 71)

Get Me There (page 72)

Check that the child follows the correct directions.

Week 7

Sentence Detective (page 74)

1. no
4. no
2. yes
5. yes
3. no

National Symbols (page 75)

1. C
2. A

A Special Day (page 76)

Check that the response includes an activity that the child would do as an adult.

What Is It? (page 77)

Check that art includes the outline of the apple in a creative way.

Shape Count (page 78)

1. 8
3. 15
2. 12

Answer Key *(cont.)*

So Many Shoes! (page 79)

1. 5; 2; 1   2. 5; 3; 7

Make a Story (page 80)

1. Story should include subtracting 6 – 2 with 4 milk cartons left.
2. Story should include adding 2 + 8, totaling 10 fish.

Try This! Answer should include the numbers 2, 3, and 5.

Next Number (page 81)

9, 10	19, 20	30, 31
13, 14	22, 23	
16, 17	28, 29	

Tic-Tac-4 (page 82)

Check that the markers are correctly placed and that there are four in a row.

Week 8

More Than One? (page 84)

1. bed   3. can
2. apples   4. nuts

Pal the Dog (page 85)

1. a dog   3. Tim's shoes
2. the door   4. He helps Tim.

Gone Fishing? (page 86)

Check that the response includes reasons to support why the child would or would not like to go fishing.

My Community (page 87)

Check that the drawing includes various community streets, houses, businesses, etc.

Make Ten (page 88)

1. 3 + 7 = 10   3. 2 + 8 = 10
2. 5 + 5 = 10

Find the Shapes (page 89)

Check that the correct shapes are circled or underlined.

Make or Break (page 90)

Check that the two numbers in each box equal to 7 when added or subtracted.

Riddle Me This (page 91)

a rainbow

Hear This! (page 92)

Check that sounds are identified correctly.

Week 9

Vowel Focus (page 94)

1. lake, rake, take   4. fame, same, tame
2. zone, cone, lone   5. hire, wire, tire
3. dive, alive, hive

A Powerful Plant (page 95)

1. B   2. A

Three Wishes (page 96)

Check that the response includes three wishes.

Flag Art (page 97)

Check that the chosen shape includes a country's flag design.

Hop Backward (page 98)

1. 3   3. 2
2. 4

Taller and Shorter (page 99)

Check that the taller and shorter objects are correct.

Problems, Problems! (page 100)

1. 4; subtract   2. 8; add

Number Sudoku (page 101)

2	4	3	1
3	1	2	4
1	2	4	3
4	3	1	2

Community Jobs Charades (page 102)

Check that each player correctly acts out the jobs.

Parent Handbook

Dear Parents or Guardians,

Have you ever wondered why states have learning standards? Teachers used to determine what they would cover based on what content was included in their textbooks. That seems crazy! Why would educators put publishers in charge of determining what they should teach? Luckily, we've moved past that time period into one where educational professionals create standards. These standards direct teachers on what students should know and be able to do at each grade level. As a parent, it's your job to make sure you understand the standards! That way, you can help your child be ready for school.

The following pages are a quick guide to help you better understand both the standards and how they are being taught. There are also suggestions for ways you can help as you work with your child at home.

Here's to successful kids!

Sincerely,

The Shell Education Staff

College and Career Readiness Standards

Today's college and career readiness standards, including the Common Core State Standards and other national standards, have created more consistency among states in how they teach math and English language arts. In the past, state departments of education had their own standards for each grade level. The problem was, what was taught at a specific grade in one state may have been taught at a different grade in another state. This made it difficult when students moved from state to state.

Today, many states have adopted new standards. This means that for the first time, there is better consistency in what is being taught at each grade level across the states, with the ultimate goal of getting students ready to be successful in college and in their careers.

Standards Features

The overall goal for the standards is to better prepare students for life. Today's standards use several key features:

◆ They describe what students should know and be able to do at each grade level.

◆ They are rigorous.

◆ They require higher-level thinking.

◆ They are aimed at making sure students are prepared for college and/or their future careers.

◆ They require students to explain and justify answers.

Mathematical Standards

There are several ways that today's mathematics standards have shifted to improve upon previous standards. The following are some of the shifts that have been made.

Focus

Instead of covering a lot of topics lightly, today's standards focus on a few key areas at much deeper levels. Only focusing on a few concepts each year allows students more time to understand the grade-level concepts.

How Can You Help?	What Can You Say?
Provide paper or manipulatives (such as beans or pieces of cereal) as your child is working so that he or she can show his or her answer.	Is there another way you can show the answer?
Have your child explain his or her thinking or the way he or she got the answer.	What did you do to solve the problem? What were you thinking as you solved the problem?

Coherence

The standards covered for each grade are more closely connected to each other. In addition, each grade's standards are more closely connected to the previous grade and the following grade.

How Can You Help?	What Can You Say?
Help your child to make connections to other concepts he or she has learned.	What else have you learned that could help you understand this concept?
Ask your child to circle words that may help him or her make connections to previously learned concepts.	What words in the directions (or in the word problem) help you know how to solve the problem?

Fluency

The standards drive students to perform mathematical computations with speed and accuracy. This is done through memorization and repetition. Students need to know the most efficient way to solve problems, too!

How Can You Help?	What Can You Say?
Help your child identify patterns that will work for increasing speed and accuracy.	What numbers do you know that can help you solve this problem?
Encourage the most efficient way to solve problems.	Can you get the same answer in a different way? Is there an easier way to solve the problem?

Mathematical Standards (cont.)

Deep Understanding

Students must develop a very good understanding of mathematical concepts. A deep understanding of mathematical concepts ensures that students know the *how* and the *why* behind what they are doing.

How Can You Help?	What Can You Say?
Encourage your child to make a model of the answer.	How do you know your answer is correct? Can you show your answer in a different way?
Have your child explain the steps he or she uses to solve problems.	Can you teach me to solve the problem?

Application

Today's standards call for more rigor. Students need to have strong conceptual understandings, be able to use math fluently, and apply the right math skills in different situations.

How Can You Help?	What Can You Say?
Encourage your child to use multiple methods for solving and showing his or her answers.	Can you explain your answer in a different way?
Have your child circle words or numbers that provide information on how to solve the problem.	What words gave you clues about how to solve this problem?

Dual Intensity

Students need to develop good understandings of mathematical concepts and then practice those concepts.

How Can You Help?	What Can You Say?
Provide practice on concepts or basic facts your child is having trouble with.	What did you have difficulty with? How can you practice that?
Have your child identify where his or her breakdown in understanding is when solving a problem.	Where can you find the help you need?

Language Arts Standards

The following charts describe the key shifts in language arts standards and some great ways that you can help your child achieve with them.

Balancing Informational and Literary Texts

Students should read and have books read aloud to them that represent a variety of texts and have a balance of informational and literary texts.

How Can You Help?	What Can You Say?
Find topics your child is interested in and then find both fiction and nonfiction books on the topic.	Since you like dinosaurs, let's find a story about dinosaurs and an informational book that tells facts about dinosaurs!
Encourage your child to know features of informational and literary texts.	How do you know this book is informational? What features does this literary book have?

Knowledge in the Disciplines

Once students reach sixth grade, they are expected to gain information directly through content-area texts rather than have the information told to them. Younger students can read nonfiction texts to prepare for this transition in the middle grades.

How Can You Help?	What Can You Say?
Talk about science and social studies topics with your child in everyday conversations so that your child learns about related words and concepts.	I heard on the news that there will be a lunar eclipse tonight. Let's watch it together so that we can see the shadow of Earth come between the moon and the sun.
Provide a variety of experiences for your child so that he or she can use them when reading about a topic. It makes the topic easier to understand.	Let's go have fun exploring the tide pools! What do you think we will see there? (*ask before*) What did you see at the tide pools? (*ask after*)

Staircase of Complexity

Students should read grade-appropriate complex texts. They may not understand the content right away, but with support and time, they will eventually comprehend what they're reading.

How Can You Help?	What Can You Say?
Know your child's reading level. Help your child find books that are at the high end of your child's reading level.	I found these three books for you to read. Which one interests you?
Read books to your child that are above his or her reading level. It exposes him or her to more complex vocabulary, sentences, and ideas.	Which book would you like me to read to you?

Language Arts Standards *(cont.)*

Text-Based Answers

Students should be able to answer questions and defend their positions using evidence from texts. This evidence can include illustrations and other graphics.

How Can You Help?	What Can You Say?
Ask your child to explain his or her answer using evidence from a book.	How do you know that? How else do you know _____?
Ask your child to look for evidence about something you notice in a book.	What evidence is there that _____?

Writing from Sources

Students should easily reference the texts they are reading as they write about them.

How Can You Help?	What Can You Say?
Have your child underline in the text the answers to questions he or she is answering through writing.	Where is the evidence in the text? How can you include that in your written response?
Provide sentence frames to help your child reference the text.	On page _____, the author says _____.

Academic Vocabulary

Academic vocabulary is a student's ability to recognize, understand, and use more sophisticated words in both reading and writing. Having a strong vocabulary allows students to access more complex texts.

How Can You Help?	What Can You Say?
Model using precise vocabulary.	I noticed you used the word _____. Could you have used a stronger word?
Provide a wide variety of experiences for your child to learn new words. These experiences don't have to cost money. They can be simple, everyday activities!	We are going to get the oil changed in the car. I want you to see if you can find the mechanic in his overalls.